Carmel Summers

Lost in the Pleiades

Lost in the Pleiades
ISBN 978 1 76109 623 5
Copyright © text Carmel Summers 2023
Cover image: a page from *Sidereus Nuncius* showing Galileo's
drawings of the stars in the Pleiades star cluster. Image courtesy of
the History of Science Collections, University of Oklahoma
Libraries. Licensed under the Creative Commons Attribute 1.0
Generic. Source: http://hos.ou.edu/galleries/17thCentury/Galileo
1610/Galileo-1610-016c-1%20%20Version%202-image/

First published 2023 by
GINNINDERRA PRESS
PO Box 3461 Port Adelaide 5015
www.ginninderrapress.com.au

Contents

Introduction	7

An artistry of stars
Learning to Fly	13
After Pleiades by Elihu Vedder	15
My Friend's Seven Sisters Bracelet	17
Landscape for Seven Sisters	19

Watching
Starry Messenger	23
Photobombing Seven Sisters	25
Job ponders the Pleiades	27
God's throne	29
Star gazing	30

Many worlds, same stars
Girls in the Sky	33
Dao Luk Kai: a fable	35
Snow Star Festival	37
Winter 1995 at Weiwera Hot Springs	39
Astronomer's Tools	40
Star Maps	42
Subaru Cluster	44
Joanna Lumley watches the Dance of Bedhaya Ketawang	47

Those insistent Pleiades
Pantoum to a Ladybird Beetle	51
Not seven dwarfs after all	53
Shortbread	55
Stozhary Villanelle	57

The Alexandrian Pleiad
1. Homer of Byzantium sings of Eurypyle	61

2. Coriambs by Philiscus of Corcyra	65
3. Lycophron's Alexandra	67
4. Hissing at Sositheus of Alexandria	69
5. Fragments of Alexander Aetolus	71
6. Aratus and the moon	73
7. Theocritus speaks on the pitfalls of love	75

La Pléiade

1. Ode to a Pierre Ronsard Rose	79
2. If our life is less than a single day	81
3. The Poet and the Massacre	83

Travels with the Pleiades

Watermelon Nights	87
The Gift	88
Paper daisies	89
References for individual poems	92
Acknowledgements	100

Introduction

> Seven are they [Pleiades] in the songs of men, albeit only six are visible to the eyes. Yet not a star, I ween, has perished from the sky unmarked since the earliest memory of man, but even so the tale is told. Those seven are called by name Halcyone, Merope, Celaeno, Electra, Sterope, Taygete, and queenly Maia. …they wheel in heaven at morn and eventide, by the will of Zeus, who bade them tell of the beginning of Summer and Winter and of the coming of the ploughing-time.
> – Aratus (ca 315–240 BCE), *Phenomena*

As long as I can remember, I have been equally fascinated and appalled by Western classical mythology: a world of heroes, villains, caring, violence, cruelty and loss. Within that mythological world, things of earth and things of the heavens reflected each other. An example of that is the Pleiades, commonly called the Seven Sisters or M45 in Western cultures, deriving their name from the Greek legend of the seven sisters, daughters of Atlas and Pleione.

The Pleiades is an open star cluster in the constellation of Taurus. It is approximately 410 light years from Earth. There are more than a thousand stars in the cluster, which appears as a cloudy concentration in the sky. The Pleiades is adjacent to the Orion cluster. With the earth's rotation, Orion appears to chase the Pleiades across the night sky.

The stars are named after their mythological counterparts: Maia, Electra, Taygete, Celaeno, Alcyone, Sterope and Merope. The Pleiades also contain stars called Atlas and Pleione. There are various Greek mythological stories of these sisters – in one, they are fleeing Orion, a Boeotian giant, who follows them across the sky. In others, they are placed in the heavens by their father for safety or after their death.

In the northern hemisphere, the dawn rising of the Pleiades occurs in spring and from early times marked the seasons for sailing and farming. By autumn, the Pleiades set in the morning and this marked the end of the harvest.

Galileo was the first person to view the cluster using a telescope. He identified and mapped thirty-six stars and published his findings in his treatise *Siderius Nuncius* in 1610. Charles Messier measured the position of the cluster in 1771 and assigned it as object M45 in his catalogue of comet-like objects. Nowadays, on a clear night away from city lights, six stars can be seen, as recorded by Aratus in 300 BCE. So why do stories based on these stars commonly refer to seven stars?

It is thought that the star called Pleione is outshone by a nearby star called Atlas, making it invisible to the naked eye. However, many thousands of years ago, these stars would have been further apart when viewed from earth, hence the seven stars of the Pleiades. Another theory is that Pleione is a shell star that changes and varies in intensity over intervals of thousands of years.

That was all I knew about the Pleiades until 2016, when I visited the information centre at Mt Stromlo Observatory on the outskirts of Canberra. I was overwhelmed by displays that illustrated the Dark Emu in the Milky Way and the Seven Sisters stories told by many Aboriginal nations in Australia. This set me on a research journey, finding stories and connections with the Pleiades across many countries and cultures – some direct, some indirect.

Then in 2017 and 2018 I attended the Songlines, Tracking

the Seven Sisters exhibition at the National Museum of Australia. I followed the seven sisters of the stories as they journeyed across Australia. This exhibition was brilliant. The artwork, the modes of storytelling, the representations, were diverse but consistent, as the story was taken up by each country and passed to the next as the sisters travelled across the continent. Pursued, they travelled from Martu country in the west, through Ngaanyatjarra lands, Pitjantjatjara and Yankunytjatjara country.

These stories, like many others in different cultures are not mine to tell. However, I was driven to respond to the stories and artwork, and the poems in this volume began. This book explores the various connections that we have with the Pleiades around the world. The name for these stars changes from place to place and time to time, but I have used the name Pleiades as a reference, as that was my starting point.

In some cases, the poems have a direct link to the stars themselves, or a response to artistic representations. I have also explored traditions based on these stars, or where the name has been applied to other endeavours, however obscure the connection.

I end this collection with a poem that reverses the journey of the Seven Sisters across our continent. I do so acknowledging that people belonged to and knew this land and its songlines tens of thousands of years before my family travelled here.

Every time I step under a clear night sky, I still look up, find the Pleiades and get lost in wonder, once again.

Carmel Summers

[Seven Sisters] is not just one songline – they travelled all around Australia. And even other people overseas know the Seven Sisters story in their own way, so it's a special story. It's not only happening here in Australia but it happened everywhere else.

– Ngalangka Nola Taylor with Kimpaya Girgirba,
Songlines, Tracking the Seven Sisters, Margo Neale ed.,
National Museum of Australia Press, Canberra, 2017

An artistry of stars

Twinkle, twinkle, little star,
How I wonder what you are!
Up above the world so high,
Like a diamond in the sky.
– Jane Taylor

Kungkarrangkalnga-ya Parrpakanu (Seven Sisters Are Flying) is one of the fabulous artworks featured in the Songlines, Tracking the Seven Sisters exhibition at the National Museum of Australia. It was created by Tjanpi Desert Weavers in 2015 using mixed media. Works range from 208 to 252 centimetres tall. The figures can be viewed at https://songlines.nma.gov.au/tjanpi/

Figures are by Angilyiya Tjapiti Mitchell and Paula Sarkaway Lyons; Elaine Warnatjura Lane and Janet Nuyunkanya Lane; Anawiri Inpiti Mitchell and Nora Nyutjanka Davidson; Janet Nyumitji Forbes and Freda Yimunya Lane; Jennifer Mintiyi Connelly and Mildred Nginana Lyons; Jennifer Nginyaka Mitchell and Belle Karrika Davidson; Claudia Yayimpi Lewis and Miriam Iwana Lane.

An enactment of the seven sisters story as told by the custodians of the Kuru Ala Seven Sisters site can be viewed at https://songlines.nma.gov.au/tjanpi/story/

Learning to Fly

After *Kungkarrangkalnga-ya Parrpakanu* (*Seven Sisters Are Flying*)

I wish you could have seen it, Mum
the way those artists wove grass, branches, raffia, fencing wire, feathers and wool
the way you taught me to cast on, twisting eight-ply around steel needles, drawing through the back of each stitch to make a firm basque
the way their arms stretched high, fingers open as if to grasp the air
the way you taught me to hold the needles, not too tightly, not too lightly
the way their bountiful breasts, outlined in yellow (my favourite colour), hung loudly and proudly – no mistaking these sisters for shrinking types
the way you bought me my first training bra and warned me of the perils of men
the way their colours blended and morphed – shades of magenta, blue, aquamarine to the ochres of earth
the way you always suggested muted tones that would match any outfit
the way their hair exploded in a tangle of unbridled wool
the way you brushed my hair and plaited it in braids so taut it hurt.
Mum, I wish you could have seen how those seven sisters rose into the night sky across the dome of the Travelling Kungarangkulpa display
and how I too, learned to fly.

Elihu Vedder painted the *Pleiades* using oil on canvas in 1885. The painting measures 61.3 by 95.6 centimetres and is held at the New York Metropolitan Museum of Art. The central figure in the painting, with her bindings broken, represents the lost Pleiad, often thought to be Merope, the only sister to marry a mortal and die. It can be viewed at https://www.metmuseum.org/art/collection/search/13070

After *Pleiades* by Elihu Vedder

Anchored on a stream of light
seven sister dance

in endless time
as tethered to the stars

as stars to them
hands entwined in strands

that snare and entangle
with starlight

in flight, but watchful
doleful, fearful

as Orion rises in pursuit
and Merope pauses

her ribbons broken
hands poised like

a lutist between notes
but her eyes

her eyes…
is it knowledge

of her future
bound to Sisyphus

in his impossible fate
each day to roll that rock uphill

to watch it fall unloosed
or did she know

how humans would learn to mark
the passage of the sisters

as a warning
for the fleet to anchor

to prepare the earth
to plant the seeds

just as Zeus in his lust
impregnates the sisters

casts them to the sky
forever fleeing

My Friend's Seven Sisters Bracelet

She chose blue enamel set in a silver band –
a place to plant those Songlines images
that swirled and swirled in her head
refusing to leave long after
the doors of the museum were locked.

Each drop of molten silver
a fragment from her life –
lonely earrings, chains that had forgotten their pendants
outgrown fashions, girlhood must haves.

Orion's stone, from the simple ring
her mother had worn for fifty years.
Seven diamonds in a cluster –
splinters from her own broken dreams.

Yarrkalpa (*Hunting Ground*) is a massive artwork by the Martumili Artists for the Songlines, Tracking the Seven Sisters exhibition at the National Museum of Australia. The artists who created the work are Kumpaya Girgirba, Yikartu Bumba, Kanu Nancy Taylor, Ngamaru Bidu, Yuwali Janice Nixon, Reena Rogers, Thelma Judson and Ngalangka Nola Taylor. Painted in acrylic on linen, it measures 300 by 500 centimetres. When viewing this artwork, I felt myself being drawn into this vivid landscape.

Yurla (Orion) is the shape-changing man who pursues the Seven Sisters.

See https://www.nma.gov.au/exhibitions/songlines to view the painting.

Landscape for Seven Sisters

After *Yarrkalpa (Hunting Ground)*

Trace the contours of the sandhills
lightly, lest you disrupt their gentle curves
the wattle, honeyed grevillea, jakapiri.
Tiptoe past the patchwork of ash, bare earth
freshly burned to nurture nature's balance
and don't startle the crafty monitor's tracks.
Edge around rocky outcrops, no need to climb
to reach water soak and course
through ground where tips of green
promise new crops and bush tomato.
Follow Wanarl Creek
near the Canning Stock Route along restored land
rich with pencil yam, bush onions, bush raisin
stretches of wallaby grass
until you find the place where the Seven Sisters rested
midst flowering plants, mulga and white coolibah.
Explore the colours – golds, reds, blues, greens
find waterholes, grasslands, township
seed and gum-producing acacias
in a landscape never constant
each dot on this vast array a richness of lifestyle
of instruction, of sharing, of generosity
and where seven sisters, long ago
sat on a hilltop as Yurla watched on, waiting…

Watching

When the blazing sun is gone
When he nothing shines upon,
Then you show your little light,
Twinkle, twinkle, all the night.
– Jane Taylor

Siderius Nuncius, which translates to *Starry Messenger*, was written by Galileo in 1610. It was ground-breaking as the first publication that described the heavens viewed through a telescope. In his work, he mapped thirty-six stars of the Pleiades and the craters of the moon.

Starry Messenger

Indeed, with the glass you will detect below stars of the sixth magnitude such a crowd of others that escape natural sight that it is hardly believable. – Galileo Galilei

Orion's constellation overwhelms me. So many points of light. And no time. The heavens. My telescope. The lens so narrow. Incessant interruptions as clouds lower and linger.

My son and daughters in their cot. In our bed Maria Gamba sleeps. A pastime I can ill afford. I draw my breath from the night sky. The stretch and fall of stars.

My naked eye. Pupil dark-adapted. Its aperture always the limit. Sometimes I can see and sometimes not. I count the stars of the Bull called Pleiades. It deceives me. Six or nine flicker in and out of my vision.

Between clouds. Waiting. Always waiting. Telescope ready. My hands tremble and I see nothing but a blur. Lose my place in the sky.

This moment when I seize my pen. Draw the first dots on my map. Six black points. I long for dark parchment and golden ink instead. I draw the large six. Mark them again with double outlines. My anchor in the skies.

Each day I grind and polish my glass. Lens convex. Eyepiece concave. Each to complement the other. Ready for night rise. The cocks are quiet. Noise from the tavern croaks like frog call in the swaddle of Brenta's shores. I wait for the Pleiades to rise.

My eyes. I blink and blink to clear them. Narrow my lids. Count the lesser stars. Map their winding passage past their larger sisters. Add the thirty-six of which I'm sure. Carefully. Preserve their mutual distances and sizes.

Knowing. Not knowing. Fearful to show my findings to the world. The vast expanse of otherness. Outside our world. But belonging. In ways I cannot know. The key to knowledge is this glass I grind and polish. Mount in its holder. Frame the lens from external light.

Even as I draw these distant stars. I know. I know there is more. Much more. How can we on earth discover all there is? The Pleiades. The sky. The moon. The sun. And how they form a whole.

Photobombing Seven Sisters

Between 1 and 5 April 2020, the planet Venus passed in front of the Pleiades when viewed from central UK at 9 p.m.

It happens. The happy newly-weds
a passer-by behind, hand raised
in V for Victory, or is his wrist flipped
for a different sign?
Zoom meetings where the cat,
always the cat, jumps on a lap
worse a laptop. It happens.
Then on 3 April 2020
Venus photobombed the Pleiades
and though this didn't cause
a traffic pileup on the M2
Britons armed with binoculars last used
for Newcastle United vs Nottingham Forest
witnessed a different Transit of Venus
as she swept across the sisters
glowing brighter than the moon.
Photobombing.
It can happen to anyone.

There are only three mentions of the Pleiades in the Old Testament. These are Amos 5:8; Job 9:9; and Job 38:31.

Job ponders the Pleiades

Lord, I am a good man. Didn't I stay fast to you when my servants brought word that my property had been burnt to ashes, my livestock stolen, my children dead, ravished by a windstorm. Your wind, Lord. And Lord, didn't I say that the Lord gives and the Lord takes away and blessed be your name? I didn't criticize you, Lord, even when boils throbbed throughout my flesh and my wife, constantly at me, at me, to curse you. There were times I wished for death to end my pain. So tell me, Lord. Help me to understand. What have I done to deserve this? But I can't find you, Lord, to tell you I am a good man. I am alone; I suffer; people mock me. Elihu tells me that pride is my sin; that I can never know more than you, Lord; never be more righteous than you. Perhaps he's right. Perhaps I should fear, not question you, Lord. The thought makes me so afraid I tremble. Then, wonder of wonders, you speak to me out of a whirlwind. Lord, you ask me where I was when you laid the earth's foundations, set stars in the sky. You ask if I could have bound the chains of the Pleiades, loosened Orion's belt, brought forth the constellations in their seasons, or led the Bear with its cubs. You ask if I have any notion of the laws of the heavens. And, Lord, I must admit, these are things beyond the reach of a mortal man like me. Lord, I admit I presumed to know too much; but now, Lord, I hardly know how little I do know. And then, Lord, you reveal to me your Lordliness and all my losses are restored, my skin smooth to touch, my sons and daughters gather round me and we gaze at the constellations of the Bear, the Pleiades and Orion and know that you alone are Lord.

The Pleiades constellation appears in the sky directly above the great pyramid of Khufu (Cheops) in Egypt at midnight of the autumnal equinox. Alcyone, the central star of the Pleiades was thought by Jehovah Witnesses to be the centre of the universe and thus, the throne of God. The theory was disowned in 1953.

God's throne

Reading the spiral inward:

von Fraunhofer with its achromatic objective lens; held close by followers of Charles Taze Russell until 1953, a theory proposed by Johann Heinrich von Mädler observing through a 95 millimetre refractor telescope made by Joseph cross the skies; signified by the finger of the great pyramid of Khufu at midnight on the autumnal equinox, around which the other stars of the Pleiades revolve, as day after day, they cross the throne of Jehovah, centre of gravity for the universe; Alcyone – site of the throne of Jehovah

......when such views were considered UNWISE

Star gazing

Here, on a quiet hill, so still my city ears
buzz with the unaccompanied sound
of distance and looking up I feel
drawn into nothingness
in the dizziness of seeing that
night sky, the extravagance
of lights that glint or glow or pulse
some veiled by shimmering clouds
others as penetrating as steel
and one that falls –
drawing me
to tumble and tumble
through that endless abyss.

Many worlds, same stars

> Then the traveller in the dark
> Thanks you for your tiny spark,
> How could he see where to go,
> If you did not twinkle so?
> – Jane Taylor

Devils Tower or Bear Lodge, is an igneous sheer monolith (laccolith) in the Devils Tower National Monument (park) in Wyoming. A Kiowa story, captured in the documentary series *Cosmos, A Spacetime Odyssey,* Episode 8, 'Sisters of the Sun', relates how seven girls became the Pleiades, where they appear directly above the monolith in winter.

Girls in the Sky

the boil and bluster of an igneous intrusion
through sediments of a forgotten sea
flow of magma pushes strata aside –
red sandstone, maroon siltstone
white gypsum, grey-green shale
iron-rich veins leaking from sandstone
molten rock rises high, chinking the surface.

the extrusion within cools
to form joined hexagonal columns
each as wide as a person is tall…

the cloak of sandstone crumbles and erodes
wind, snow, waters scour the earth
layer after slow layer
where Belle Fouche River
carves the edge of Bear Lodge Mountain.

there, late at night
from a clear mid-winter sky
those lost girls glow and glitter.

In Thailand, the story of Dao Luk Kai, the seven chickens, is told as a singing game. It is used to teach the virtues of love and caring.

Dao Luk Kai: a fable

Listen, children, listen and learn the love of a mother, the love of children, the love of angels, the earth, the sky – where we look on this clear, clear night at seven sparkling chick stars, Dao Luk Kai. Hear this story how an old man and old woman living at the forest's edge reared a hen and seven chickens – even the naughty youngest – Jiw – who danced and played and caught the eyes of crow and might have been lost to crow's cruel claws and thrusting beak but for his mother's outspread wings. So they lived; old man, old woman, mother hen, seven chicks until one day, a passing monk on his Dhutanga journey stopped and asked for food – of which there was none. Overheard by mother hen, the old man and old woman wondered which of the chicks should be cooked to offer food to the monk. Heart pounding, hen raced back to her chicks, told them to hide, that she would sacrifice herself for their sake. Ah, with love, with love, she threw herself into the flames to scorch her feathers to prepare herself to be cooked. 'Not without us!' called Jiw – and seven chicks braved the scorching fire to comfort their mother. The heavens, in awe at this devotion, swooped, clutched the chicks from the biting flames, drew them to the skies, where, children, they shine to remind us –

                    to love.

Qoyllur-Rit'I, or the Snow Star Festival, is held in the Sinikara Valley in Peru every year. The festival celebrates the reappearance of the Qullqa star cluster (Pleiades) in the sky, which signifies the beginning of the harvest. The festival also pays homage to the legend of the visitation of Christ in a burning bush.

Snow Star Festival

In the Andes, when the snow stars shine in June
A time to gather crops, and hail new year
Until that day a herder sought rare cloth

A cloth too fine to shirt a simple boy
A fabric only archbishops could use
In the Andes, when the snow stars shine in June

The archbishop sent soldiers, priests and guns
To seize the boy and ask how could he dare
A simple herder should not seek that cloth

Instead of a mestizo boy, there stood
A man whose clothes shone brighter than the sun
In the Andes, when the snow stars shine in June

Before their eyes the holy man transformed –
A burning bush and image of the Christ
On the day a herder sought to buy fine cloth

It's now a place and time where pilgrims go
For harvest rites and some to seek the Christ
In the Andes, when the snow stars shine in June
On the day a simple herder sought some cloth.

Weiwera Hot Springs is a thermal area north of Auckland, New Zealand. In Maori, *Matariki* is the name for the Pleiades. In 2021, Jacinda Ardern, the prime minister of New Zealand, declared Matariki Day as a public holiday and day of remembrance to honour those who have been lost since the last rising of *Matariki*. The first sighting of *Matariki* and *Puanga* at dawn marks the winter solstice.

In Maori, *Puanga* is the name for Rigel, *Tamanuiterā* for the sun, *Takurua* for Sirius and *Raumati* for summer.

Winter 1995 at Weiwera Hot Springs

early frost
a chill that clings to skin all day
but here at Weiwera
steam lingers like winter breath
exhaled from midday pools
on this day as clear as cat's eyes
after a dawn where *Matariki* and *Puanga* first appear
Tamanuiterā turns from his northern sojourn
to leave his winter wife *Takurua*
and travel to the house of his summer bride
but for now
the languid waters
the steam and the chill

Astronomer's Tools

I wish there were a telescope
strong enough to chart your distant moods.
Binoculars with their wider field of vision
are too slow to follow your movements.
My naked eye simply falls short.

Once I thought I'd mapped your planispheres,
made apt observations on your point of view
as befits mother to child
but now   drawn by far-off nebulae
your orbit skews.

Last month I watched the moon's eclipse
not seeing a greater occultation
much closer to me.
The aftermath of a meteor shower
continues to rain.

Light pollution clouds my night sky
my vision falters.
A friend told me not to worry.
But can a mother?
Ever?

I eat my morning toast and jam.
See your bed   again   unused.
In my mind I play your voice
as it used to be.
Unbroken.

When night falls
I'll be here
waiting to catch the flicker and flash
of your teenage equatorial coordinates
as you go star-hopping.

Star Maps

Some claim there are echoes of the heavens in the vast reaches of China's landscape – a Pleiadian map inscribed in the guise of the Xiaoling Mausoleum. Here, in the tomb of the Emperor Hongwu, men have built monuments that chart the heavenly Pleiades. The same configuration of stars can be found in nature at the Seven Star Park in Guilin, four stark peaks on Putuo Hill, three on Lunar Hill. Underground are caverns that have been inscribed with words by poets for more than 1,300 years.

>   the shape of seven
>   promise of eternity
>   entombed
>   pattern for aesthetics, or
>   reflection of the stars

There are a number of stories in Japan that relate to the cluster of stars called Subaru, which also means to govern or gather together. Each tanka or haiku represents a different Subaru story. Subaru are sometime called Houki Boshi or brush strokes, the jewels that entice the sun (Amaterasu) to rise, signifiers for the seasons for agriculture or love-making, or a drunken Subaru fleeing a proprietor (Sakamasu Boshi) for refusing to pay for his drinks. The six stars of the emblem for Subaru vehicles reflect the name taken when five corporations amalgamated to form Fuji Heavy Industries Ltd.

Subaru Cluster

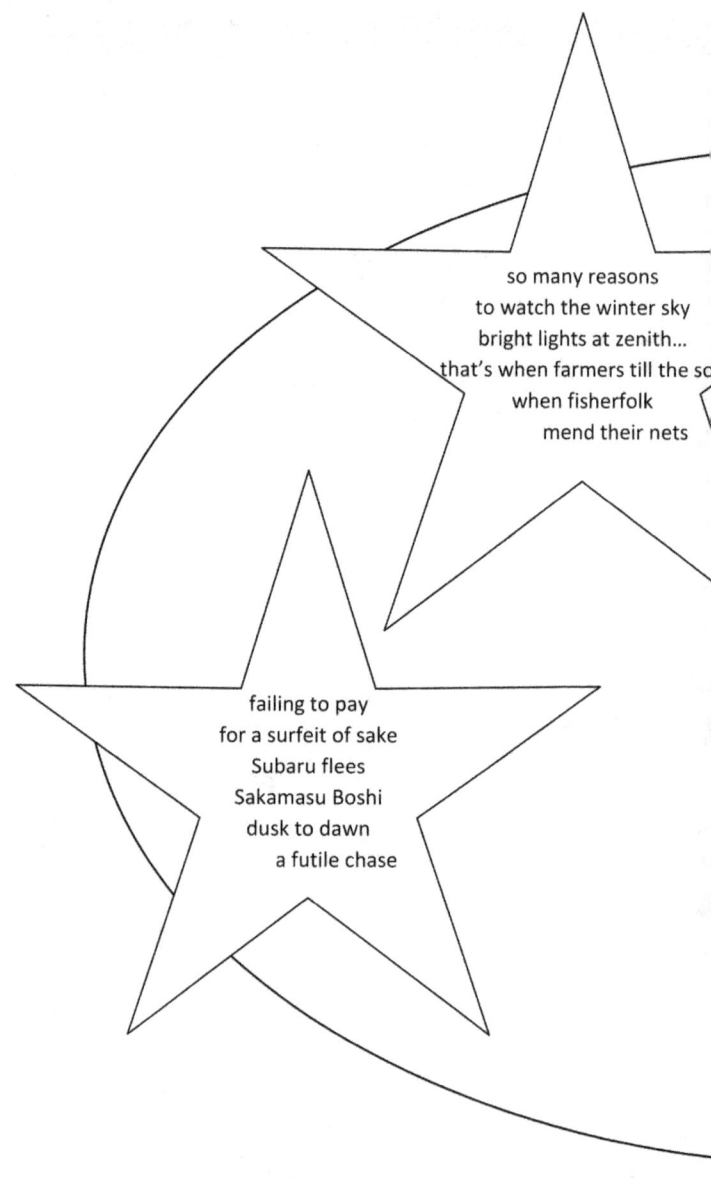

so many reasons
to watch the winter sky
bright lights at zenith...
that's when farmers till the so[il]
when fisherfolk
mend their nets

failing to pay
for a surfeit of sake
Subaru flees
Sakamasu Boshi
dusk to dawn
a futile chase

sparkling jewels
entice Amaterasu
to warm the earth –
year after year
the churn of chill
and riches

Subaru
seven daubs of light
on an ink sky

five companies merge
to build the perfect car
its six star emblem
borrowed from the skies...
how we travel
on this earth

moon in the east
Subaru in the west
best time for making love

The Javanese sacred dance *Bedhaya Ketawang* means 'The Dance of the Heavens'. The original dance was said to be performed by seven beautiful nymphs created from seven sparkling gemstones. It is only performed on special occasions within the royal palace. One of the configurations during the dance represents the position of the seven stars of Lintang Kartika (the Pleiades). Joanna Lumley is an English presenter, well-known for her softly-narrated documentaries of cultures around the world.

Joanna Lumley watches the Dance of *Bedhaya Ketawang*

If Joanna Lumley were here
in Java – together with invisible film crew
she would surely be invited to the inner reaches
of the palace by Surakarta's sultan
perhaps to mark his coronation
more likely, his anniversary.

If Joanna Lumley were here
she would oh! and ah!
at the glitter of gold thread
gold arm bands, gold bracelets
gold tiaras with their gleam of seven stars
oh! oh! so much gold!

If Joanna Lumley were here
she would want to finger
the silken scroop of gowns
of nine dancers indistinguishable
in movement, makeup and costume
but even she must keep her distance.

If Joanna Lumley were here
she might whisper in undertones
as the hands of the dancers
weave a dance of their own
and song and music play
in a stretch of hours.

If Joanna Lumley were here
she might tell us about this sacred
dance from the heavens
how it tells a love story
between the King of Matarama
and the Queen of the Southern Sea.

If Joanna Lumley were here
she might murmur
how the dancers form the shape
of the Pleiades constellation
and other secret moments
in the dance of Bedhaya Ketawang.

And then tiptoe away.

Those insistent Pleiades

In the dark blue sky you keep,
Often through my curtains peep
For you never shut your eye,
Till the sun is in the sky.
– Jane Taylor

The Pleiades in Norse mythology were called Freyja's hens, (*Freyjuhoena*) and after Christianity took hold, were renamed Mary's hens (*marihøne*), the name also given to ladybird beetles because of their seven spots and red outer wings, as Mary was often represented wearing a red cloak. The seven joys and sorrows of Mary were also represented by the seven stars on her cloak. The nursery rhyme 'Ladybird, Ladybird' dates back to the sixteenth century with Germanic origins and is thought to relate to religious persecutions at the time.

Pantoum to a Ladybird Beetle

this red-cloaked bug with seven spots, approx.
cocinellidae to those who know her well
steals her name from stars called Freyja's hens
and lays her eggs to feast on aphid throngs

cocinellidae to those who know her well
full filmy wings rest under glossy shells
she lays her eggs to feast on aphid throngs
her struggle to survive a daily chore

full filmy wings rest under glossy shells
your house is on fire, your children are gone
her struggle to survive a daily chore
where lurk her seven sorrows, seven joys

your house is on fire, your children are gone
Christianity displaces old Norse gods
where lurk her seven sorrows, seven joys
except Anne who hid under the warming pan

Christianity displaces old Norse gods
she steals her name from stars called Freyja's hens
except Anne who hid under the warming pan –
this red-cloaked bug with seven spots, approx.

The Brothers Grimm tale of 'Snow White and the Seven Dwarfs' is based on northern German stories relating to the movement of the sun, moon and stars.

Snow White (the sun) is driven away by the Wicked Queen (the full moon) and spends the winter half-year with the seven dwarfs (the seven stars of the Pleiades).

The rectangular shape in Gemini, viewed only at certain times of the year, represents the glass coffin of Snow White.

Interestingly, brown dwarfs have been identified in the Pleiades cluster.

Not seven dwarfs after all

Narrative arc or cycle lit by stars?
Does Snow White flee along an unpathed forest
find refuge in the house of Happy, Bashful and company
or do the Pleiades sink at the spring solstice
holding the sun as close as solar flares allow?
Spring turns to summer, to autumn
until the winter solstice hunkers down
the wicked moon floats across the sky
passing the Pleiades not once, but thrice, bearing
a bright red ribbon to lace her bodice
a comb with teeth laced to kill
an apple, half green, half rosy
half wholesome, half lethal.
Too lethal.
January over Germany brings despair.
In the north eastern sky after sunset
a glass coffin in the constellation of Gemini.

This poem is based on a coincidental relationship to the Pleides, the name for which is *ülker,* in Turkey; a name it shares with the Ülker Company, manufacturer of the Pötibör biscuit. This was derived from Petit Beurre biscuits in France, which were derived from Scottish shortbread. The first Ülker Pötibör biscuit was manufactured in 1944.

Shortbread

Shortbread is on my mind this morning. Its soft crumble on my tongue. Butter that oozes past my nostrils. Secretes in hidden corners of my body. So many varieties to choose from. The robust Scottish variety. The grit of rice flour. Butter that lingers on the lips. Was this the inspiration for the *petit-beurre* of Nantes in 1886? So very French. Dotted precisely with 24 indents lined in a grid of 4 by 6, fifty-two identical teeth fluting its edges. Each biscuit exactly 65 mm long, 54 mm wide, 6.5 mm thick and 8.33 grams. Plus or minus nothing. And a delicate infusion of butter like the first drag of nicotine after a month of good intentions. Which brings me to the *pötibör*. Alas. Palm oil. No butter.

Stozhary was a cinematic festival held in Kyiv between 1995 and 2005. Named and themed after the Pleiades (Stozhary, which literally means a hundred-fold embers), the festival was held over seven days with a jury of seven awarding seven prizes.

Stozhary Villanelle

The stars go waltzing out in blue and red – 'Mad Girl's Love Song',
Sylvia Plath

A festival where actors congregate
seven-coloured banner flying high
designed for inspiration and debate.

A time to mingle and to celebrate
a hundred glowing embers in the sky
a place where film-lovers congregate.

It's novelty they're striving to create
extending genres others might not try
designed for inspiration and debate.

Excitement mounts as judges nominate
categories for which the actors vie
a time when film juries congregate.

Eager innovators ruminate
a range of new techniques some might apply
designed for inspiration and debate.

It runs five times, a grand conglomerate
an experiment not hard to justify
a fete where film-makers congregate
designed for inspiration and debate.

The Alexandrian Pleiad

The Alexandrian Pleiad is the name taken by a group of seven tragic poets in Alexandria in the court of Ptolemy II Philadelphus. They named themselves after the seven stars of the Pleiades. Many of their works have been lost or only fragments survive. This section contains a poem to represent the achievements of each of these poets:

> Homer of Byzantium
> Philiscus of Corcyra
> Lycophron
> Sositheus of Alexandria
> Alexander Aetolus
> Aratus
> Theocritus

Homer of Byzantium is variously credited with forty-four, forty-seven or fifty-seven works, the only remainder of which is the title of his poem 'Eurypyleia'. He was also called Homer the Younger to distinguish him from the author of *The Odyssey* and *The Iliad*. He wrote at the beginning of the third century BCE.

1. Homer of Byzantium sings of Eurypyle

was his name blessing or curse, this Homer-not-Homer?
did he write on a parchment scraped

from sheep skin that his wife would
rather be kept for sturdy shoes

than wasted in those endless words, written
right to left, then left to right, the way

an ox turns when a field is ploughed?
so he labours, tragedy after tragedy.

how many times does he reach the end?
forty-five, forty-seven, fifty-seven…

and did he know that all would be lost
except his name, and rumours that he

or another, wrote the tragedy, *Eurypyleia*?
but which tragic Eurypyle did he choose?

was this Eurypyle one of fifty
all daughters of Thespius

raped in a single night by Hercules?
or was it the maenad Eurypyle

one in Dionysus' fan club
(swap miniskirts for fawn skins)

who, god-intoxicated, drew milk
from streams, wine from earth

honey from the wood of ivy
suckled wolf cubs and fawns alike

impervious to fire, snakes, iron
yet slain, defending her god

at the hand of Morrheus?
or was it another Eurypyle

a queen of the Amazons?
did she hack off her right breast

freeing her arm to shoot an arrow at
her enemies (and there were many)?

did she lead her women to pillage Babylon
or Ninus? did she kill her sons

or spare them for their father to raise and
sire future generations?

did she die mid-battle or
grow old weeping for her lost women?

Sometimes, truth can disappoint.
Sometimes, it's better not to know.

Philiscus of Corcyra wrote forty-two dramas, of which nothing is known. He was also a priest of Dionysus. Choriambic hexameter verse is attributed to him.

2. Coriambs by Philiscus of Corcyra

a choriambic poem that has six feet
would be a dreadful form to write within
more limp than glide, more stammer than a song
a weary tread of feet, a doleful dirge...

dum-da-da-dum, dum-da-da-dum, dum-da-da-dum...

this pulse could mark the beating of a drum
a sullen trudge of broken, blear-eyed slaves
an ominous, repeating undertone
iambic will outdo it any day

da-dum, da-dum, da-dum, da-dum, da-dum

Of the 20 poetic works by Lycophron, only fragments remain, except for 'Alexandra', which tells the story of the Trojan War, as told by the prophetess Cassandra. 'Alexandra' is reputed to be the most obscure and disjointed poem written in this tradition and may or may not be correctly ascribed to him. This is a found poem based on random words selected from A.W. Mair's translation of 'Alexandra'.

3. Lycophron's Alexandra

unchartered winds rush and wash the land
garlanding the back of steep hills
where clashing armies are entombed

a second nameless dominion taken
as Cassandra points her finger
her voice a surety of wars ahead

though her future, Lycophron's past
and present, unwanted
for who would have believed

their own country overrun
by unrepentant Romans, bearing bitter arrows
as surely as Troy taken in the past

but who is she, this Cassandra/Alexandra?
who speaks of dragon's fire, lions, dophins
and the sweet song of a nightingale

in the same breath as slaughter of children
rape and pillage, gods and armies
in constant flux and lack of reason

enshrining her maidenhood to
the last, and from a prison cell
screaming her unrelenting Siren's song.

Sositheus of Alexandria is best remembered for an incident, recorded by the biographer Diogenes, when he criticised the well-known poet Cleanthes and was hissed off the stage. Only fragments of his drama and pastoral plays remain.

4. Hissing at Sositheus of Alexandria

Who would dare to front a teacher
especially a teacher like Cleanthes
unless you are
a guest poet reading in the theatre
(Cleanthes' own space indeed)
and utter the words:
Driven by Cleanthes' folly like dumb herds…

and Cleanthes standing there, gobsmacked
perhaps even with his mouth ajar
not finding any words to say
       but the audience did –
such booing
such hissing
that Sositheus slinks from the stage

and when he apologises
some time later
Cleanthes retorts that since the very gods –
Dionysus, Heracles –
had been ridiculed by poets
it would be absurd for him
to take umbrage.

Only fragments of the poetry of Alexander Aetolus remain, one of which is titled 'Helena'. The subject of the poem is unknown.

Helena was a painter in the fourth century BCE, known for her painting of the battle of Issus.

5. Fragments of Alexander Aetolus

He may have written about   a different Helena
probably the Trojan beauty   but
with   only   fragments   who can say?

I prefer to think of another Helena
who should have been famous
in her own time and place

a creative   not destructive   Helena
an artist renowned for her epic
painting of the battle of Issus

one of Alexander's excursions –
he was called 'Great' but
alas   this Helena

didn't make the cut, when
Pliny the Elder catalogued
women artists of antiquity

in his *Natural History*
– despite her famous painting
but maybe   just maybe

this Helena was lauded
in a poem
by Alexander Aetolus

Aratus was a didactic poet and astronomer whose major extant work is 'Phenomena'. 'Phenomena' is a massive poem that describes a huge number of celestial bodies and proposes a means of predicting weather by the stars and moon. The Crater Aratus on the moon and the minor planet 12152 Aratus are named in his honour.

6. Aratus and the moon

Scan [the moon]…each month. When quite bright her hue, forecast fair weather; when ruddy, expect the rushing wind; when dark stained with spots, look out for rain… But if halos encircle all the Moon, set triple or double about her or only single – with the single ring, expect wind or calm; when the ring is broken, wind; when faint and fading, calm; two rings girding the Moon forebode storm; a triple halo would bring a greater storm, and greater still, if black, and more furious still, if the rings are broken. Such warnings for the month thou canst learn from the Moon. – Aratus, 'Phenomena' [799]

What would he have thought, had he known
that a crater on the moon
would be named after him?
That moon whose phases he described
waxing, waning, horned and haloed.

A single ring, faint and whole for calm days ahead
if broken – wind
two rings for stormy weather
three for a greater storm
fiercer still if black
furious if the moon's three rings broken.

Aratus, a lunar impact crater
its image snatched by Apollo 15
the reverse of my granddaughter's
sand bucket castle on the beach
at Skegness on the far side of the earth
where storm clouds bank to block the rising moon.

Theocritus has been called the creator of Ancient Greek pastoral poetry. He wrote pastoral bucolic poetry, idylls and mimes as well as lyric and epic poetry. He was a friend of Aratus, to whom he addressed 'Idyll VI. A Country Singing Match', translated by J.M. Edmonds, on which this poem is based.

7. Theocritus speaks on the pitfalls of love

Aratus, my friend, my patient friend
to speak of the pitfalls of love
are Daphnis and Damoetas
herdsmen with voices more eloquent
than mine, they leave a poet wasted.

First Daphnis sings and swings his hips
to imitate the sea-nymph, Galatea
casting apples to seduce a weary version
of the Cyclops feared by many
but to her, a plaything
as she throws apples to his dog
taunting, teasing, testing
will he, won't he…
but see how fast she would run if he does.

Damoetas takes the stage, assumes
the Cyclops grating laugh
as he presumes to look away
unmoved, unmoving
but for a niggling thought
that his dog might be won over
by gifts of apples, but in the end
he knows by playing hard to get
she'll come running, begging, pleading

For such a catch Cyclops thinks himself –
straight teeth, curly locks
good looks – which he sees
from his reflection in a glassy sea –
so long as he spits in the water first
to ruffle the surface
and squints.

And satisfied they know the pitfalls of love
the herdsmen
        Daphnis and Damoetas
            kiss.

La Pléiade

A group of sixteenth-century French Renaissance poets took the name La Pléiade, based on the Alexandrian Pleiad and also named after the Pleiades star cluster. The main members were Pierre de Ronsard, Joachim du Bellay and Jean-Antoine de Baïf.

Inspired by *Ode a Cassandre: Mignonne, allons voir si la rose* by Pierre de Ronsard (1524–1585). Pierre de Ronsard is also the name given to a rose.

1. Ode to a Pierre Ronsard Rose

New to gardening, when
I opened the catalogue –
Treloar Roses, 2017
106 glossy pages
Three pictures abreast
In colours that shimmered.

Each bud and blossom
A precise shape with no hint
Of black spot or powdery mildew.
And when I found you on
Page 73, I knew
I had found the perfect rose.

However, even love has its season…
Flowers wither, aphids thrive
You hunger for more and more
Food and constant tending
And, sharper than a shrew's tongue –
Your thorns.

After *Si nostre vie est moins qu'une journée* by Joachim du Bellay. Du Bellay was one of the founders of La Pléiade and a champion of the French language and introduced classical forms, including sonnet and odes. His later romantic poetry was said to be inspired by an affair with a married Roman lady called Faustine.

2. If our life is less than a single day

Sometimes, a poem's title can mislead you into thinking
Of a life in the context of just one day and not eternity
As was intended. But even so, the prospect of ashes
To ashes – and all that – at the end of one's allotted time
Can lead one to consider if it was really worth
The effort, what was the point
And why it seemed so hard at times
To find the opportunity for fun.

What a difference love makes –
As du Bellay found, when working with his Cardinal
In Rome, and met Faustine, immortalised
As Columba or Columbelle, until interrupted
By her jealous husband which may have precipitated
His return, alone, to Paris.

Jean-Antoine de Baïf was a follower of the court of Cartherine Medici. His sonnet *'A la Roine Mere Roy'* praised the massacre of St Bartholomew, but he moderated his views in a later poem, *'A Monseigneur de Lansac'*.

3. The Poet and the Massacre

In name, King Charles, but everybody knew
Medici was the queen who ruled his hand.
They crept by stealth, and struck by her command
To slay the Huguenots, who scarcely drew
Their swords before they found it was too late.
The dead piled up in city, town and field –
Such waste because religion couldn't yield,
Till thirty thousand people met their fate.

One time, it was a poet's place to write
To praise a king who led his men to death.
Now thoughts have changed, and attitudes as well
I use a pen, not sword, to set things right.
The horror of those times has soured my breath
And fills my nights with screams of those who fell.

Travels with the Pleiades

> As your bright and tiny spark
> Lights the traveler in the dark,
> Though I know not what you are,
> Twinkle, twinkle, little star.
> – Jane Taylor

Watermelon Nights

long, hot summer nights
air draws close and clings to your pores
not a touch of breeze
to unstick the clamminess of your clothes
your dad brings home a watermelon
bought from the back of a roadside truck
your mother hacks it into chunks
and you all stretch out on the cool grass
in your own backyard
hills hoist in silhouette
against the lights of your silent house
you bite the melon, dribbling juice
chomp down to the white of rind
strain the seeds hard against your tongue
then compete with your brother and sisters
to see who can spit the farthest
until sated with sweetness
you lie on your back, play 'find the stars'
point to the pointers of the Southern Cross
the red blinking eye of the star you call 'beetle juice'
the saucepan above it, your knowledge of that vast array
scant
not knowing this is the belt of Orion
as he pursues across the rim of sky
a splotch –
like a watermelon's soft white inner seeds –
stars whose names you do not know.

The Gift

About to turn away
I see a peach, just one, that has escaped
possums and cockatoos.

Other peaches…the late flowering tree
on the secret side of the house
my brother perched up high

tossing fruit to me below
the silken scent of ripeness
rising into sunshine

and he asked me, this brother from boarding school
on his home holiday
about my school work

explained the mysteries
of the universe, stars
and constellations

a listening and understanding
I'd not before experienced
but lasted almost fifty years.

The gap when he was gone.

This single peach.

Paper daisies

1.

Crossing the continent in 1992
my mother-in-law doesn't know…
as all along that snaking railway
she sketches Sydney blue gums
crumbling rifts of sandstone
velvety bracts of flannel flowers, banksia
and heath, flashes of purple break o'day
without knowing whose land she travels –
Eora, Dharug, Wiradjuri, Wongaibon.

2.

Her ticket enough, no passport
to let her cross from Barindji
to Barkindji and Danggali and Wiljali
western plains fading into night
while she touches colour to outlines
of salt bush and dead blackbox trees
inserts the fractured landscapes
of mining towns into her sketchbook.

3.

She doesn't know as she captures
the city of churches, the yellow surprise
of *hibbertia tenuis*
that she travels the country
of Ngadjury, Nukunu, Kaurna
collecting, not Banggaria, Wirangu,
but white paper daisies, red dodonaea
and purple patterson's curse.
She remarks in her unpolished hand
the absence of trees, wonders how
such large boulders came to lie
in the Nullarbor flatness
without thought of meteors
or flight of seven sisters.

4.

She notes
in Mirning and Myenganyatjara country
a landing strip, hospital, school, scattered houses
and the disgrace of two old boxes
sweltering unshaded jails…
Her train spares
no time for reflection, the landscape
through the window
morphs from desert
to apricot-coloured watsonias
green and red kangaroo paw, winged wattle
banksia petrolaris
and *diplolarena grandiflora*.

5.

She is mesmerised
by a maze of pink paper daisies.
Foliage obscures their roots
deep in the soil of Icathaa
Kalaamaya, Balardung and Wajuk.

6.

She doesn't know, as I did not,
how long ago this land lay below
the shallow Eromanga Sea
teeming with life
whose soulless shells
still line the empty shores
how even now, Kati Thanda waits
fifteen metres deeper
than the top of the ocean
how one day that sea may return
sooner or later
in ways that we don't know
to cleave our land
to separate our cities

to drown those paper daisies.

References for individual poems

'Twinkle, twinkle, little star'
Written in 1805 by Jane Taylor
https://www.poetryfoundation.org/poems/43200/twinkle-twinkle-little-star

'Learning to Fly'
Songlines, Tracking the Seven Sisters, Margo Neale ed., National Museum of Australia Press, Canberra, 2017
https://songlines.nma.gov.au/tjanpi/
https://songlines.nma.gov.au/tjanpi/story/

'After 'Pleiades' by Elihu Vedder'
https://www.metmuseum.org/art/collection/search/13070

'Landscape for Seven Sisters'
Songlines, Tracking the Seven Sisters, Margo Neale ed., National Museum of Australia Press, Canberra, 2017
https://www.nma.gov.au/exhibitions/songlines

'Starry Messenger'
Galileo Galilei *Siderius Nuncius*, Venice, 1610. Albert Van Helden (trans) 1989, University of Chicago Press, Chicago, Illinois
Machamer, Peter, 'Galileo Galilei', *The Stanford Encyclopedia of Philosophy* (Summer 2017 edition), Edward N. Zalta (ed.), https://plato.stanford.edu/archives/sum2017/entries/galileo/

'Photobombing seven sisters'
https://astronomynow.com/2020/03/29/planet-venus-photobombs-the-pleiades-seven-sisters-1-5-april/

'Job ponders the Pleiades'
https://www.biblestudytools.com/job/

'God's throne'
http://www.quotes-watchtower.co.uk/god_s_throne_-_pleiades.html

'Girls in the Sky'
Devils Tower Monument, National Parks Service: https://www.nps.gov/deto/index.htm
A Living Monument: Devils Tower Plants: https://www.google.com/url?sa=t&rct=j&q=&esrc=s&source=web&cd=&ved=2ahUKEwj-kt3l-M_uAhXF6XMBHf3fDg8QFjABegQIExAC&url=http%3A%2F%2Ffiles.cfc.umt.edu%2Fcesu%2FNPS%2FUWY%2F2011%2F11Heidel_DETO_plant%2520interp_publications_Appendix%2520A.pdf&usg=AOvVaw2A9mFpiMUJWiW_edVY5kNd
Geology information: https://www.nps.gov/deto/learn/nature/tower-formation.htm
https://en.wikipedia.org/wiki/Devils_Tower
Kiowa story of the maidens and the bears: Documentary series: *Cosmos, A Spacetime Odyssey*, Episode 8, 'Sisters of the Sun', 27 April 2014

'Dao Luk Kai: a fable'
http://www.rspg.org/fabel/doc3.htm (translated using Google translate)
Thaiculture.com (http://www.prapayneethai.com/th/amusement/north/view.asp?id=0370)

'Snow Star Festival'
https://www.enigmaperu.com/blog/everything-you-need-to-know-about-qoyllur-riti/

'Winter 1995 at Weiwera Hot Springs'
https://www.newzealand.com/au/matariki/
https://www.stuff.co.nz/national/the-detail/300109206/the-detail-a-comeback-for-waiwera-hot-pools

'Star Maps'
http://thehiddenrecords.com/china.php
https://www.chinahighlights.com/guilin/attraction/seven-star-park.htm
https://www.guilinchina.net/attraction/seven-star-park.htm

'Subaru Cluster'
https://www.fivestarcars.com/blog/2014/august/11/origin-of-the-name-subaru.htm
Renshaw S.L., Ihara S. (2000) 'A Cultural History of Astronomy in Japan'. In Selin H., Xiaochun S. (eds) *Astronomy Across Cultures. Science Across Cultures: The History of Non-Western Science*, Vol. 1. Springer, Dordrecht.
https://doi.org/10.1007/978-94-011-4179-6_13

'Joanna Lumley watches the Dance of Bedhaya Ketawang'
https://asiasociety.org/video/bedhaya-epitome-javanese-dance
https://cosmoquest.org/x/365daysofastronomy/2015/07/26/jul-26th-pleiades-and-javanese-culture/

'Pantoum to a ladybird beetle'
https://manticore.press/2016/05/21/freyas-hens/
https://en.wikipedia.org/wiki/Coccinellidae
https://www.catholiccompany.com/content/the-seven-sorrows-of-mary
https://catholicism.org/the-seven-joys-of-mary.html
https://en.wikipedia.org/w/index.php?title=Ladybird_Ladybird&oldid=1082893293

'Not seven dwarfs after all'
Barber, A. & Chamberlain, M. (1982) 'Snow-White', *Tales from Grimm*. Angus & Robertson (60–71)
E. Moraux, J. Bouvier, J.R. Stauffer and C. Cuillandre, (2003) 'Brown dwarfs in the Pleiades cluster: Clues to the substellarmass function', *Journal of Astronomy & Astrophysics*, DOI: 10.1051/0004-6361:20021903.
https://www.aanda.org/articles/aa/pdf/2003/12/aa3257.pdf
deutschlhttps://www.deutschlandfunk.de/fruehe-vorlaeufer-der-sternzeit-schneewittchen-als.732.de.html?dram:article_id=490169andfunk.de (translated using Google Translate)

'Shortbread'
www.ulker.com.tr
https://en.wikipedia.org/wiki/Petit-Beurre
https://www.ulker.com.tr/en/meet-ulker/our-history

'Stozhary Villanelle'
Wikipedia contributors. (2020, July 14). Stozhary. In *Wikipedia, The Free Encyclopedia*. Retrieved 06:06, 26 April 2021, from https://en.wikipedia.org/w/index.php?title=Stozhary&oldid=967598397

'The Alexandrian Pleiad'
Wikipedia contributors. (2018, August 16). Alexandrian Pleiad. In *Wikipedia, The Free Encyclopedia*. Retrieved 02:33, 24 April 2021, from https://en.wikipedia.org/w/index.php?title=Alexandrian_Pleiad&oldid=855113177

'Homer of Byantium sings of Eurypyle'
The Oxford Classical Dictionary. London: Oxford University Press, 1949
https://www.historymuseum.ca/cmc/exhibitions/civil/greece/gr1060e.html

W. Smith (ed.). (1870). *Dictionary of Greek and Roman Biography and Mythology.*
https://web.archive.org/web/20070406022828/http://www.ancientlibrary.com/smith-bio/1620.html

'Coriambs by Philiscus of Corcyra'
Wikipedia contributors. (2020, October 13). Philiscus of Corcyra. In *Wikipedia, The Free Encyclopedia*. Retrieved 02:32, 24 April, 2021, from https://en.wikipedia.org/w/index.php?title=Philiscus_of_Corcyra&oldid=983312802
1911 Encyclopædia Britannica/Choriambic Verse. (2016, September 11). In *Wikisource*. Retrieved 02:35, 24 April, 2021, from https://en.wikisource.org/w/index.php?title=1911_Encyclop%C3%A6dia_Britannica/Choriambic_Verse&oldid=6424238

'Lycophron's Alexandra'
A.W. Mair, G.R. Mair. (1955). *Callimachus, Hymns and Epigrams; Lycophron; Aratus*
https://books.google.com.au/books/about/Alexandra.html?id=NprxCQAAQBAJ&redir_esc=y
Classical Texts Library: Lycophron – Alexandra.
https://www.theoi.com/Text/Lycophron/Alexandra.html
Wikipedia contributors. (2021, January 12). Lycophron. In *Wikipedia, The Free Encyclopedia*. Retrieved 02:31, 24 April 2021, from https://en.wikipedia.org/w/index.php?title=Lycophron&oldid=999970134

'Hissing at Sositheus of Alexandria'
R.D. Hicks (ed.) *Diogenes Laertius, Lives of Eminent Philosophers,* Ch. 5: Cleanthes
https://www.perseus.tufts.edu/hopper/text?doc=Perseus%3Atext%3A1999.01.0258%3Abook%3D7%3Achapter%3D5
1911 Encyclopædia Britannica/Sositheus. (2014, May 8). In

Wikisource. Retrieved 02:41, 24 April 2021, from
https://en.wikisource.org/w/index.php?title=1911_Encyclop
%C3%A6dia_Britannica/Sositheus&oldid=4885649

'Fragments of Alexander Aetolus'
W. Smith (ed). (1870). *Dictionary of Greek and Roman Biography and Mythology*.
https://web.archive.org/web/20070406022828/http://www.ancientlibrary.com/smith-bio/0120.html
Women in World History: A Biographical Encyclopedia. *Encyclopedia.com*. Retrieved 16 April 2021, from https://www.encyclopedia.com/women/encyclopedias-almanacs-transcripts-and-maps/helena-fl-after-333-bce

'Aratus and the moon'
Classical Texts Library: Aratus – Phenomena.
https://www.theoi.com/Text/AratusPhaenomena.html
Wikipedia contributors. (2021, April 12). Aratus. In *Wikipedia, The Free Encyclopedia*. Retrieved 04:09, 24 April, 2021, from https://en.wikipedia.org/w/index.php?title=Aratus&oldid=1017403697
http://www.scientificlib.com/en/Astronomy/SolarSystem/Moon/AratusCrater.html

'Theocritus speaks on the pitfalls of love'
Wikipedia contributors. (2021, February 21). Theocritus. In *Wikipedia, The Free Encyclopedia*. Retrieved 02:49, 24 April 2021, from https://en.wikipedia.org/w/index.php?title=Theocritus&oldid=1008012400
Classical Texts Library: Theocritus Idylls 5–11.
https://www.theoi.com/Text/TheocritusIdylls2.html#6

'La Pléiade'
Wikipedia contributors. (2021, March 1). La Pléiade. In

Wikipedia, The Free Encyclopedia. Retrieved 07:55, 24 April 2021, from https://en.wikipedia.org/w/index.php?title= La_Pl%C3%A9iade&oldid=1009625142

'Ode to a Pierre Ronsard Rose'
Treloars Rose Catalogue, 2017
https://ocw.mit.edu/courses/global-languages/21g-321-childhood-and-youth-in-french-and-francophone-cultures-spring-2013/readings/MIT21G_321S13_ronsard.pdf
https://lyricstranslate.com/en/mignonne-allons-voir-si-la-rose-my-sweet-let-us-see-whether-rose.html
Wikipedia contributors. (2021, April 6). Pierre de Ronsard. In *Wikipedia, The Free Encyclopedia.* Retrieved 08:08, 24 April 2021, from https://en.wikipedia.org/w/index.php?title=Pierre_de_Ronsard&oldid=1016384027

'If our life is less than a single day'
Si nostre vie est moins qu'une journée, (*L'Olive augmentée*: 113) by Joachim du Bellay translation:
https://www.poetryintranslation.com/PITBR/French/DuBellayPoems.php
Wikipedia contributors. (2020, December 6). Joachim du Bellay. In *Wikipedia, The Free Encyclopedia.* Retrieved 08:35, 24 April 2021, from https://en.wikipedia.org/w/index.php?title=Joachim_du_Bellay&oldid=992682469
https://www.britannica.com/biography/Joachim-du-Bellay

'The Poet and the Massacre'
Wikipedia contributors. (2021, January 5). Jean-Antoine de Baïf. In *Wikipedia, The Free Encyclopedia.* Retrieved 01:25, 25 April 2021, from https://en.wikipedia.org/w/index.php?title=Jean-Antoine_de_Ba%C3%AFf&oldid=998541806
Wikipedia contributors. (2021, April 16). St Bartholomew's Day massacre. In *Wikipedia, The Free Encyclopedia.* Retrieved

01:29, 25 April 2021, from https://en.wikipedia.org/w/index.php?title=St._Bartholomew%27s_Day_massacre&oldid=1018063413

Roberts, Yvonne. 'Jean-Antoine de Baïf and the Saint-Barthélemy', *Bibliothèque d'Humanisme et Renaissance,* Vol. 59, No. 3 (1997), pp. 607–611, Retrieved 25 April 2021, from http://www.jstor.org/stable/20678289

'Paper Daisies'
The AIATSIS Map of Indigenous Australia:
https://aiatsis.gov.au/explore/map-indigenous-australia
My mother-in-law Era Summers' travel diaries

Acknowledgements

I wish to thank the wonderful poets in Canberra and Sydney who have patiently and generously given their time and energy in workshopping the poems in this collection, especially the Tram Stop Poets and Arboretum Poets in Canberra. I particularly thank my sister and fellow poet Anne Benjamin, who provided much critical input and positive encouragement. I am also indebted to Anne Benjamin, Penelope Layland, Hazel Hall and Kathy Kituai for their thoughtful comments and critiquing of this work. I also thank Tjanpi Desert Weavers for feedback on my poem based on their beautiful artwork.

Always, always, Rob and Carol, Helen, Laurence and Emily, whose love sustains me.

'Paper Daisies' was awarded 2nd place in the June Shenfield Poetry Award 2020
'Photobombing Seven Sisters' was published in the *Canberra Times,* August 2021
'My Friend's Seven Sisters Bracelet' was published in *Orbit Journal,* UK, March 2022
'Subaru Cluster' was published in *Kokako*, 2022

www.ingramcontent.com/pod-product-compliance
Lightning Source LLC
Chambersburg PA
CBHW071020080526
44587CB00015B/2440